To Rachel, the budding radio engineer—BB
To the memory of George Kemp—RBC

This Edition is published by Backpack Books, a division of Barnes and Noble, Inc.

Text © Beverly Birch 1995
Illustrations © Robin Bell Corfield 1995
Designed by Herman Lelie

Produced by Mathew Price, Ltd.
The Old Glove Factory
Bristol Road
Sherborne
Dorset DT9 4 HP
England

2001 Barnes & Noble Books

ISBN 0-7607-2663-9

Printed and bound in Hong Kong

10 9 8 7 6 5 4 3 2 1

MARCONI'S
BATTLE FOR RADIO

Beverley Birch
Illustrated by Robin Bell Corfield

BACK PACK BOOKS

At the ship's rail the three men hunched down in their heavy winter coats. Icy winds blasted from the open sea, and they had to squint through sea spray as the ship nosed into the narrow neck of water toward the harbor.

At once they saw the great cliff. From its snowy rock, a tower gazed ahead to the harbor and back across the wilderness of the Atlantic Ocean where icebergs drifted like vast white mountains.

Was this the place where they could make their dream come true?

They did not ask the question aloud. Not a single person on that ship knew why they had sailed from England ten days ago, why they had crossed 2,000 miles of freezing winter seas to reach this distant corner of Newfoundland.

It was a secret, and they must keep it so.

The problem was that these three men were famous. People liked reading about them; at the slightest excuse reporters would take a ship or a train to track them down.

The three men weren't ready for that. Not yet.

And so they waited for the ship to dock, huddled in their overcoats, impatient to step ashore. First went Guglielmo Marconi, and then his two assistants, George Stevens Kemp and P. W. Paget, and behind them a strange assortment of luggage hauled from the ship's hold and piled on the dock.

Wooden crate after wooden crate, a huge
basket big enough to hold a large animal, but
light for its size, and long metal cylinders.

Across the ocean, on a faraway tip of
England, a group of specially chosen people
also waited, also impatient, to hear that
Marconi and his team had landed.

First, they must find the right place to work. Somewhere high. Somewhere with a view straight across the ocean toward England.

Somewhere like that hill at the harbor channel.

They all had a good look at it, particularly Kemp—for Kemp would have to launch the balloons and kites packed in that large basket. He trudged around, plodding through drifting snow. Was there room enough to anchor ropes for holding kites against this roaring wind?

Marconi and Paget hurried in and out of the old buildings. A splendid shelter for their equipment!

It was Friday, December 6, 1901 when they climbed that hill. It was bitterly cold and getting colder, and all the time they fought the fear that the vicious weather would never let them do what they had come to do.

We know their thoughts because they wrote about this day and the days that followed in their diaries. You can still read them today, more than 90 years later, and see how each of them felt.

Soon that hilltop echoed to the sound of pickaxes, as local men hacked at the frozen earth and heaved plates of metal around. Marconi, Kemp, and Paget raced to get their equipment safe and dry under shelter.

As they worked away on that icy hill, the twentieth century (the 1900s) was not yet two years old. There was no television or radio in 1901. Using electricity at all—for lights or machines—was still very new.

But people had learned to send a message by electricity—as long as a wire carrying the electricity joined the sender to the receiver.

No wire—no message.

That is, not until Marconi came along.

That was why Marconi was already famous. To the watching world he had conjured a kind of magic in the air above the earth. He had sent messages vibrating *through the air without wires*. No physical link joined sender to receiver, and Marconi's messages winged their way at the speed of light—186,286 miles each second!

Scientists had said it was not possible. They knew all about the mysterious, invisible electrical waves, and to think of sending them more than a few miles was just a dream!

It wasn't. Marconi had done it. He had sent the electrical vibrations into the air, as far as he wanted. He had caught them back from the air, just as he chose.

That was six years before, at home in Italy.
He'd only sent them from one end of an attic
room to the other, watched by his mother.

But months followed, while he fiddled with pieces of wire and metal. He struggled to make the vibrations jump longer distances between the equipment that sent them, the *transmitter*, and the equipment that caught them, the *receiver*.

His brother Alfonso became his constant helper, guarding the receiver, raising a shout of delight each time the surge of electricity sent by Marconi from the attic started the receiver's buzzer tingling.

First, Alfonso carried it down from floor to floor of the big house. Then out onto the sunny terrace. Finally, armed with a white flag to wave when the buzzer sounded, he marched away through fields and orchards.

One day Marconi had been trying out two metal plates wired to his transmitter. He arranged them first one way, then another, in the hope that he could make the signals jump farther. One metal plate lay on the ground.

By chance, he held the other in the air.

A sudden victorious shout! A frantic waving of Alfonso's flag! Far out of sight beyond a ridge, the buzzer   had buzzed.

The vibrations   had flown across hills!

A vast jump—just because of a metal plate held high in the air! Over the next six years Marconi worked and worked to get the arrangement right. He changed the air plate for a copper wire and called it an *aerial* (also called an antenna). The ground plate was the *earth*.

Week by week, month by month, he sent the electrical vibrations (now called *radio waves*) over longer stretches of land and water. By 1901 they could travel 224 miles.

Now Marconi faced the challenge of the Atlantic: 2,000 miles of unbroken water.

Again scientists said he could not succeed. They believed that radio waves moved in straight lines. The earth was curved, so (they said) radio waves traveling any distance would shoot out into space. The earth's curve between America and England made the bulge of the ocean like a water mountain 150 miles high!

But secretly Marconi prepared—first, a new radio station at Poldhu on the southwest coast of England, with a towering ring of poles to carry the aerials high into the air.

Next he explored a map of the world, tracing
a line from the coast of England westward,
across the Atlantic Ocean. He found the east
coast of America, and searched for the best
place to build a second radio station. There
must be nothing but unbroken sea between
the two.

Cape Cod. There, on the piece of land
jutting out into the sea. Marconi and his team
crossed the ocean and set to work. Slowly, the
new radio station rose into the air—a ring of
gigantic masts, just like Poldhu.

Then, disaster! Vicious winds tumbled the masts at Poldhu like matchsticks. The Poldhu men drew deep breaths, and began again.

But then gales roared through the aerials at Cape Cod and left a heap of broken wood and tangled wires.

So Marconi came to the snow-swept hill in Newfoundland named Signal Hill, bringing kites and balloons. His two grand Atlantic stations were in ruins, but it would not stop his dream.

Signal Hill also faced straight across the sea to England.

In England the team had rebuilt Poldhu, with lower masts to carry the aerials. These would send out the radio waves.

On Signal Hill, Marconi, Kemp, and Paget would try to catch them with aerials flown in the air on the balloon.

And now they were setting out the delicate equipment Marconi would use. The device to show whether radio waves had crossed the ocean was tiny—a narrow glass tube, no bigger than a thermometer. Inside were finely ground filings of different metals.

Usually the filings rested loosely in the tube. But if electricity reached them, they clung together or "cohered," giving the device its name—a *coherer*. There was also a little tapper attached—a tiny piece of metal to knock the tube and shake the metal filings loose again.

The coherer was linked to the aerial. When an electrical vibration touched the aerial, a burst of electricity ran down the wire to the filings in the tube. These would stick together and let the electricity pass across them—they formed a *switch*, switching electricity "on." At once the tapper would knock the filings loose and the electricity would switch "off" again.

But when no vibrations reached the aerial, the metal filings remained loose and the electricity stayed "off."

Usually Marconi connected the coherer to a Morse code machine. This tapped out short and long bursts of electricity as short and long sounds to show letters of the alphabet, or punched them as dots and dashes on paper. But at Signal Hill he worried that radio waves traveling all the way from Poldhu might arrive too weak to work the Morse machines.

Instead, he connected a telephone earpiece to the coherer; his ear might hear a click as each electrical pulse arrived and the metal filings clung together.

Trails of wire linked everything together, and led outside.

From there, Kemp would fasten one wire to a flying kite or balloon to form the aerial. Another wire linked the coherer to the metal plates that the local men had buried in the ground outside—these were the "earths." The process was called "grounding."

Through Sunday they worked on, testing, adjusting, testing again.

Monday came and went. The weather grew darker and fiercer.

Tuesday dawned. It was wet and foggy. But to their delight, the winds were milder—calm enough to risk launching a kite. It swooped and twisted, and Kemp ran to and fro—a guide rope loosened here, tightened there.

One whipped free and they rushed to trap and anchor it. A sudden slackening of the rope as the kite fell, then too sharp a wind tug, and a thick rope might snap like thin cotton thread!

The ropes held, and they had the kite safely in the air.

It was time to notify Poldhu.

They went down to the town and sent the
message to England on the cable telegraph
that lay along the bed of the Atlantic. Each
day, for three continuous hours, over and over
again, Poldhu must send out the same radio
signal: the letter "S" in Morse code—three
short dots. On Signal Hill they would try to
catch it.

Wednesday roared in with storms, but they
refused to let the weather stop them now.

They carried out the metal cylinders and released the hydrogen gas into one huge balloon. It began to inflate, swaying slowly off the ground.

Kemp wrestled with the guide ropes. The winds tugged at them, frantic, and the balloon tossed into the air, shuddering and vibrating.

Marconi lifted the earphone. Storm electricity crackled and hissed. The wind howled and the cliff thundered to the angry rhythm of the sea. How could he hear radio signals in all this?

Across the ocean in Poldhu the Morse code operator pressed a long lever—tap, tap, tap. At each tap, electricity jumped between two metal balls with a crash and a blinding blue spark. Out along the wires the vibrations traveled, away and over the wintery sea.

Could Marconi—2,000 miles away— possibly catch that signal a moment later?

On Signal Hill the balloon snapped at the ropes, watched anxiously by Kemp. Nothing in Marconi's ear but storm and wind.

Twelve o'clock came and went. One o'clock. Two o'clock.

Click click click!

Or was it?

Outside, Kemp used all his strength to tighten the ropes and hold the swaying monster balloon steady. If the aerials ripped off, they would have to start all over again.

Crack! The ropes snapped and the balloon shot into the air, lost among the clouds.

Now it was too dark and they were too exhausted to go on.

Thursday broke colder and grayer, with lashing rain. They decided to try a kite this time. They had six of them. If they lost these, they would lose the battle.

The first kite wheeled and swooped like a wild bird frantic to get free, and they fought to stop it from plunging against the cliff.

Paget was outside now. Kemp and Marconi took turns at the earphone.

Snap! The wind won. The kite whipped up and vanished in the fog.

Out came the second kite, and up into the air, nearly taking Paget with it.

Marconi bent over the table, straining to hear. As the gale tossed the kite like a feather, the aerial kept changing height above the land and so changing its chance of catching any signals. It could never work in these miserable conditions!

Minutes ticked by. Not a single click in the earphone.

Was there something wrong with the instruments? Something wrong at Poldhu? How would they *know* if the problem was at Poldhu?

Paget hauled at the twisting kite, desperate to hold it steady at one height. The wind flung it away from him, higher.

A sudden click in Marconi's ear. He crouched over the earphone. The tapper striking the coherer! Electricity spurting down from the aerial!

Something was coming.

Three sharp clicks—close to each other. Unmistakable. The three dots of the Morse "S"! From Poldhu.

Silence.

He passed the earphone to Kemp. Kemp
listened. Nothing. Only the crackle of
the storm.

Click click click. Kemp *did* hear them!

They called Paget, but Paget was somewhat
deaf and heard nothing.

They listened again.

The kite soared upward and suddenly it was
the right height to catch the waves. Three
clicks in the earphone, then three more …
S-S-S-S … a whole series of them!

But still they kept the secret from the
world. Just one more try. Just to be sure!
  Hailstones and hurricane winds fought them
the next day. Yet through it all came the
dots—faint, fading as the kite circled, but
always coming again, reaching them over
and over.

Now they could let the secret out.

They told the newspapers on Saturday, eight days after landing on Newfoundland. In no more than the twinkling of an eye, radio signals had traveled across the world!

And so those days of struggle against Atlantic gales have gone down as one of the great landmarks in our history.

There were many years of difficult work
ahead before they could give us the kind of
radio we have now—with voices or music from
anywhere in the world at the push of a button
or the turn of a knob.

But those were the beginnings—those icy
days on Signal Hill when Marconi, Kemp,
and Paget plucked the first "S" from the air—
and proved to the world that it could be done.

The rest is another story ...

Today, we can get information and entertainment by radio from anywhere in the world, straight into our homes. We can call for help across vast distances. Radio is a lifeline for anyone at sea, or in the air, or in any place where there are no wires to link them by electricity or telephone to the rest of us. Even the depths of the ocean and outer space can now be reached.

Before the beginning of the story in this book, there were many years of work on radio by many people in different places. And after Marconi's triumph, there were still years of work ahead, to give us the type of radio we now have.

It took Marconi and his team another year of work in Canada before they could successfully send signals back across the Atlantic Ocean, from Nova Scotia to England. They did not really know how radio waves traveled, and it was not for another twenty years, in the 1920s, that they found out enough to properly control the radio waves.

Then Marconi and other scientists had to learn how to control the lengths of the radio waves (called wavelengths). They had to develop better equipment for sending the radio waves (the transmitters) and better equipment for receiving the waves (the detectors and receivers).

A much better detector than Marconi's coherer was invented, called a thermionic valve. Eventually, this development meant that spoken words and music could be transmitted, and not just Morse code. Radio programs to entertain people began to be broadcast in the 1920s. And all the time, work continued on sending radio signals over longer distances. Short-wave radio was developed, and in 1948 the transistor radio was invented. That was the beginning of the kind of radio we enjoy and use now.

The Science Stories Books
by Beverley Birch

Benjamin Franklin's Adventures with Electricity
Illustrated by Robin Bell Corfield

Marconi's Battle for Radio
Illustrated by Robin Bell Corfield

Marie Curie's Search for Radium
Illustrated by Christian Birmingham

Pasteur's Fight against Microbes
Illustrated by Christian Birmingham